Ministering with the Angels

Experiencing the Supernatural

Written by Belinda Owens

copyright@BelindaOwens2020
All Rights Reserved

Ministering with the Angels

Keep my eyes open

    We were visiting in Mississippi when we had an open night in our schedule. We had been told of services taking place in Brandon, Ms. The services were being held by a minister in what was a Baptist church. The service was very anointed from the beginning. Worship was intense and you could feel the presence of God.

    As I stood there worshiping the Lord I closed my eyes and once again I asked God "Let me see the things unseen". I had been asking Him to show me what was happening in the spirit realm as we were worshipping.

All of a sudden I could see three regular sized angels show up on the left side of the platform. Then I turned and there appeared a huge angel about 15ft tall standing on the right side of the platform. As I watched him he opened his mouth wide and fire shot out of his mouth and went across the platform hitting the front row of people and It covered the people on the floor that were up front worshipping. As this was happening such an intense worship fell starting in those areas. I could see what looked like tongues of fire dancing on their heads and the more intense their worship became the bigger the tongues of fire would grow. It would grow until there was a huge ball of fire dancing and reaching all across the front and it would shoot back toward us and other people. Then there would be a huge tunnel of fire shoot straight up through the roof and then fire would start building all over again. I wanted to close my eyes and fall on the floor in worship but I had asked God to let me see! I had actually been begging Him to let me see. So I stood and watched while praying!

Jesus walks in

The worship was right in sync with what I was seeing. All of a sudden I sensed Jesus was coming into the room. I said in a soft prayerful voice, "You are coming now aren't you? You are going to show up!!!" The worship leader started singing, "He is a consuming fire!" and I saw a white bright light start down the center aisle. I knew it was my Jesus! I turned and watched as He walked down the center aisle straight to the front. His robe was so bright and white it sparkled with silver sparkles. I wanted to crumple to the floor! I had begged to see more and now was not the time to close my eyes! Jesus sat down on the steps that lead up to the platform to the right of the pulpit. He watched the crowd and turned his head slowly. As he turned his head toward a particular person, the evangelist would start prophesying to that person. In awesome detail the minister prophesied of what was going on in that person's life. I watched this go on for several people. Jesus would look at the people and zooming in on one particular person and the minister would just start reading that person's life! While the minister would be prophesying to them Jesus was just setting there in such peace, watching. I had NEVER experienced anything like this before! If I could have come out of my body from excitement it would have happened then! Needless to say since that night things have been different. There has been a great intensifying of God's presence. What I would feel after praying and worshipping for 30 minutes was now coming immediately. There was such an increase of the Spirit of God. I think once you have experienced the Kingdom in operation it becomes easier to function in that realm.

Serving a Real living God!

After experiencing that in Mississippi I am thinking, how can it get any better than that!

We were to speaking at Burning Man Ministries in Brownsville, Texas. (The worship is always awesome there.) God's presence shows up on a regular basis and it is so wonderful.

I was setting toward the back worshipping and again I asked the Lord "let me see the things unseen". God started giving me a word for Bro. Gary (the leader of Burning Man). Rusty asked me to come up and share before he ministered so I went up and shared the word the Lord had given me. That God was a consuming fire and about the huge angel I had seen in Mississippi that stood on the right side of the platform. And I shared the word to Bro. Gary. Rusty then ministered. After he was finished he asked for those who wanted prayer to come forth and we would pray over them. Several came forward and Rusty, myself, Bro. Gary and several others prayed over them.

We then became aware that if you walked pass the right side of the platform there was an extreme presence of God in that one location. It would literally make your feet melt under you. So I grabbed Rusty's hand and a friend's hand nearby and pulled them up to that spot. We all became so intoxicated we could hardly stand and had to grab a chair. I walked back up to the spot and stood to the side of it as close as I could without falling from the presence of God. I then caught a glimpse of an angel standing there. About that time Bro. Gary said "There is an angel standing here," as the power of God's presence knocked him into the wall! Bro. Gary said, "Come on! Anyone wanting to experience this presence of

God come up here and stand right here now!" Every single person who came forward experienced God in a powerful way! Not one person did not have a reaction to what was standing there. One young man about 6ft tall was knocked to the floor on his hind end like someone swept his feet out from under him. He couldn't get up and burst out in holy laughter! From young children to older adults everyone who walked up to that location was over whelmed with the presence of our God! When we left the building that night people were still crawling up to that area feeling the very presence of a true and living God! You might say, "Why?" Why would this happen? Well let's see, to prove to those there that God is real.

I lay in bed still awake at 2:49 a.m. just blown away that God had gotten so physical with us! We could literally feel the messenger He had sent. There have been many times where man encountered an angel. In John 5:4 the angel troubled the water in the pool. Or Acts 12:7, " and behold, the angel of the Lord came upon him and a light shined in the prison: and he smote Peter on the side, and raised him up." The bible is full of accounts similar to what happened to us. God is getting very physical with His bride we just have to be a willing vessel for Him to work through.

All I can say after this…..Lord I want more of YOU! God is no respecter of persons He will give you all of Him you want…. Just ask Him for "more"!

Ministering Angels

    Have you ever noticed when you get still that your head will be noisy for a little while but it eventually dies down? As those thoughts and events finish running thru your head and quiet sets in. That's one of the best times to hear the Father. Still yourself and listen. Listen to what He is speaking over you.

    I remember a few years ago after I had laid in bed and all was quite I fell asleep. After awhile I awoke to the most beautiful singing. As I listened it was coming from the foot of our bed. Trying to be still and take a look I raised my head and there at the foot of our bed was an angel singing the most beautiful song. It was in another language, not

English. I remember the peace I felt as this angel ministered over us.

In Zephaniah 3:17(KJV) it says "The Lord thy God in the midst of thee is mighty; he will save, he will rejoice over thee with joy; he will rest in his love, he will joy over thee with singing."

I believe angels are sent to minister to the heirs of salvation. Hebrews 1:14, "Are not all angels ministering spirits sent to serve those who will inherit salvation?"

We need to get over the shock or surprise when heaven sends angels to help us. I once heard Cindy Jacobs say, "We must get used to the angels showing up so that we can minister with them and not just be awe struck." I think there has been an over caution by some saying "don't worship the angels!" Which we don't, but we shouldn't be rude and ignorant of how the heavens function. God created them for a reason. Let's release them to minister with us. We need their help. I would love to wake up every day having the angels sing over me. That should not be an oddity but a normal happening!

God Seekers

I hope you have been seeking the Father for more of the Kingdom! God is stirring his children and His kingdom is open for us to have as much of Him as we want.

The first time I heard of "Seeker friendly" churches I thought they were churches that made it easy for you to tap into the mighty power of God! I had no clue they were churches that made a person comfortable when they attended. Comfortable in the sense that sinners would not feel uneasy setting in the pew. If we fail to bring a person to a point of seeing their need for Jesus then we have failed. When God fills the house there is such "awe" that you will want to fall down before Him with great reverence. When sinners are comfortable in God's house it is no longer God's house, it has become just a house.

We had just returned from a trip into Mexico and on this trip I experienced something I have never experienced, but have been praying for, for some time. Sometimes God wants to see if you are hungry enough to pursue Him.

God allowed an angelic visitation in our room in Texas. Usually when I sense an angel in the room when I open my eyes I will catch a glimpse of it then it disappears. This time God allowed the angel to stay even though I opened my eyes and even when I asked him his name. Through that experience we saw many people touched by God in our Texas meeting as well as the Mexico meeting and people we had contact with on our way back to Missouri. I look for these visitations to increase within those who position themselves in a place to be used in that manner. It is for us to seek after God to know Him and to know His ways. Like I said earlier I have sought God for some time for more intimate encounters with Him and the Heavenly Host.

Divine Appointment

As we traveled thru Texas I had someone text me a link to listen to a minister named Shawn Bolz. As Rusty and I were listening to Shawn Bolz speak on the YouTube video Rusty said, "Is this the man that Papa Jack (Jack Taylor) mentioned to us while we were in Florida?" I replied I didn't know but I would text Papa Jack and ask him. So I texted Papa Jack but as soon as I sent it Rusty said "Aren't they in Texas ministering this weekend?" I didn't know for sure so I looked it up and yes they were. We realized we were going to pass about 1 mile from them (Jack & Friede Taylor) in New Braunfels, TX. I texted Papa Jack's son

Tim and asked if they were in service and he said yes they were to just come on in! Long story short Rusty and I ended up on the floor in New Braunfels, TX, on our way to Mexico.

A Powerful Prayer

As I was laying there on the floor I heard Mama Friede praying over me. In her deep German accent she prayed, "God give her all of you that her body can handle!" I felt the spirit of the Lord just flood my body as she prayed over me, "God, give her all of you that her body can handle!" It is amazing what God can do to a person in just a few minutes in His almighty presence. He can change hearts, bring healing; even change your whole attitude. We got up from the floor after soaking in God's wonderful presence. We had lunch together with Papa Jack & Momma Friede and then continued on for Mexico.

An Angelic Encounter

After being in Mexico we came out to stay with some friends there in the Valley, Pastor's Gary and Patty Wilhite. They have been such good friends to us over the years and keep a room available for us to rest in when we are down that way.

About 4: 00 a.m. on Sunday morning I awoke to see about a 9 foot angel standing on Rusty's side of the bed. He was so big and he had a clay looking pot in his hands. The pot was about 3 foot tall. He would take and scoop up out of this flowing substance and pour it over me & Rusty as we lay on the bed. He continued to do this over and over. I said to him "Hey! You are still there and I can see you! You didn't disappear!" as he continued to pour.

The next thoughts in my head were "Lord, don't let Rusty wake up!" Because usually when he does they disappear. Well he kept right on sleeping and I continued to watch.

Then all of a sudden I saw what looked like a water pitcher above us. It was glowing as if it were on fire. It had liquid inside it that looked like melted gold. It tilted over and poured on us from above then it disappeared as I heard Momma Friede's voice say just as if she had been in our room, " God give her all of you that her body can handle!" and right at that moment a book appeared over us.

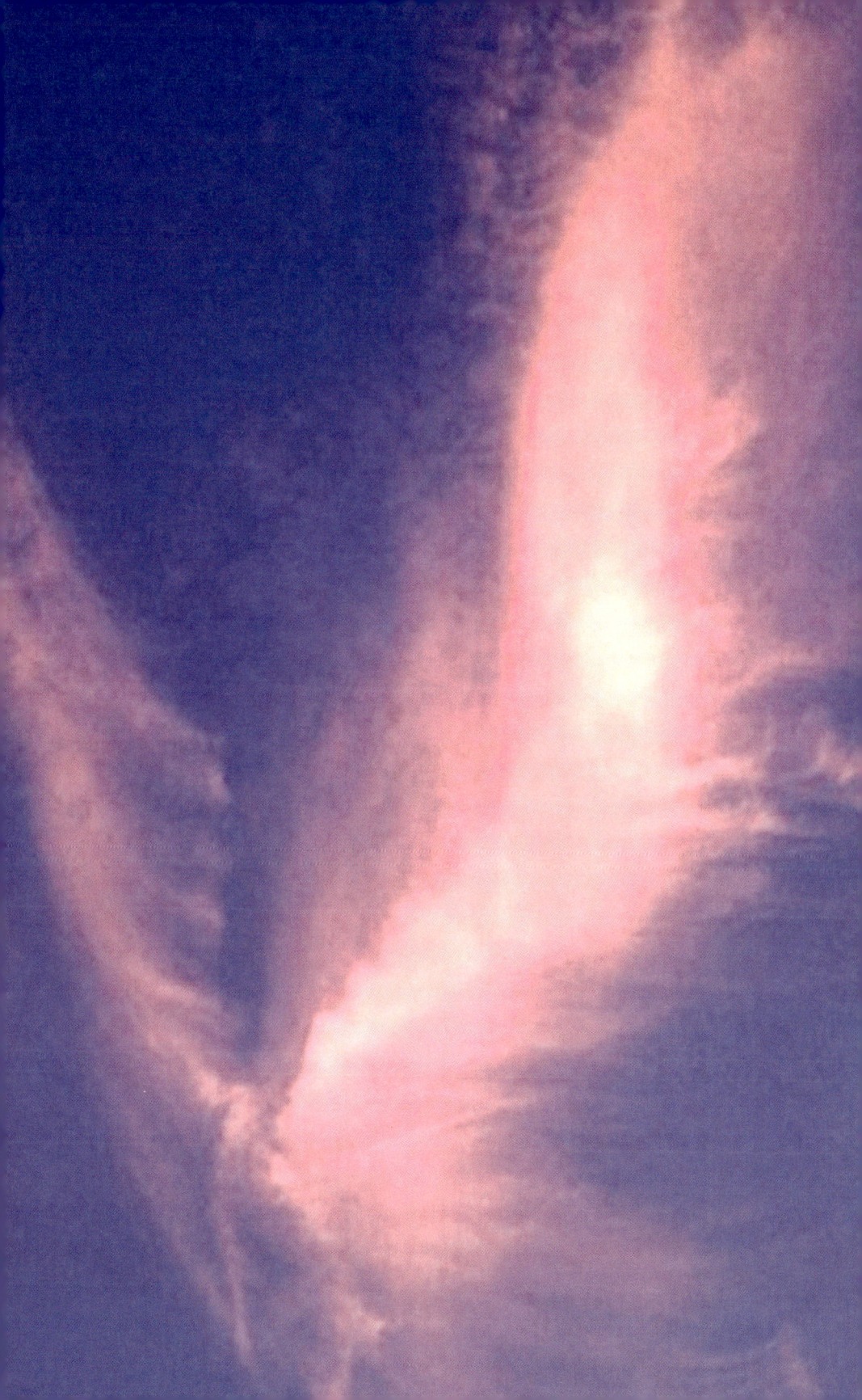

Boom! God, Shackalaka!

The book was red and as it opened light shot out of it so bright I could no longer see the book except for the very edge of red on the sides. I then heard a male voice, with a lot of authority say "BOOM! God, Shackalaka! BOOM! God, Shackalaka!" over and over. It was a voice that I would think the elders in the throne room crying "Holy, Holy!" would sound like. "BOOM! God, Shackalaka!" it repeated with great authority. The angel continued to pour out of the pot over us as I heard this. I finally reached my phone and looked up the word "Shackalaka." It is an ambiguous word but is used in a meaning of "One who wants to go higher" or "People who want to go higher" and another place it is used for when a basketball makes a goal, BOOM, and the *rim rattles "Shackalaka". I was hearing "BOOM, God Shackalaka!" I couldn't see who was saying it, they were somewhere beyond the book.*

I felt the presence of God so strong it was as if my body was glued to the mattress. The heaviness of His glory was upon me! I was trying to grasp all of it I could! Drink it in!

Impartation

In a little while it started to lift and I asked God, "Can this be imparted?" And He said, "Yes it can." And I immediately saw a vision of me, standing in front of people, praying for them and repeating, "BOOM! God! Shackalaka!" as the presence of God fell on the people.

I then asked the angel standing by the bed still pouring liquid on us out of the 3 foot clay pot, "What is your name?" He said "I am called "Stay Still, the one who pours it out." I then looked up "Stay Still", and found the scripture when God told Moses to "Stand still and see the salvation of the Lord". And the one, "Be still and know I am God." Then I looked up "the one who pours it out" and the results were in some religions there is one who is anointed to use holy designated vessels to pour out offerings unto the Lord. Needless to say I was so over joyous with this visitation I had been allowed to experience!

That morning I was able to share at Pastor Gary's church about the visitation and the angel pouring it out over us. We saw God's presence come over people blessing them in a mighty way. God doesn't give something to us for us to just keep it for ourselves. We are to impart what is given.

We went back into Mexico and I was able to share there as well and again God's presence fell upon the people. The director of the ministry there in Mexico told me after the service as tears were still streaming down his face that he wished he could speak in tongues. I asked, "You don't?" And He said that he had asked but still hadn't spoken in tongues (like in Acts 2). So we laid hands on him right there and he began to speak in a heavenly language as tears rolled down his face. It was an awesome time that began on the floor in Texas. God is so good and He will meet you *with what level of relationship you desire from Him. As for me, I just became hungrier then ever! I want so much more!*

What do Angels look like?

Over the years I have seen angels that look like men and have no wings. I have been asked if all angels have wings and the answer is no. Even the scripture says that we may entertain an angel unaware. Hebrews 13:2 (KJV), "Be not forgetful to entertain strangers: for thereby some have entertained angels unawares." So no, not all angels have wings. I have seen angels that look like females just like some look like males. I have seen angels that range from 3 feet or less to angels that were extremely tall, 30' feet tall.

I saw one angel in our bedroom one night. I awoke to see him floating beside me. He was about 3ft tall and had more muscles than a body builder. He was very buff and not only that but he was a bluish color. No white robe, he and what he had on were the same color, a light bluish color. When I *saw him he placed a scroll to my ear and then he hit the end of it knocking it into my head. There are spiritual things that take place that do not fit into our human way of thinking. Just remember when you function in the supernatural you are functioning without the restraints of this world. John 4:24 (KJV), "God is a Spirit: and they that worship him must worship him in spirit and in truth." The first angel I ever saw was a female looking angel who was floating right above me as I slept. When I woke up she was glowing as if she were all white with a black light reflecting on her. She just floated right out the window when I saw her.*

Partnering with the Angels

One night we were ministering in a service. Toward the end we had people come forward for prayer. As we ministered to the people the Spirit of the Lord intensified. As I was laying hands on the people I was moving backward to move on down the line and continue praying. As I backed up I bumped into the person behind me. As I turned to apologize for bumping them there was no one there. Although I had physically felt it as I bumped into them the space behind me was clear, no one was behind me.

Growing up, I can remember my dad who was a minister who functioned in miracles, healing, and deliverance. One night as we were setting around the table after a service he said, "I know that y'all have seen me reaching back with my hand as if I am feeling

something as I am preaching." He said "I can feel an angel standing with me as I preach." I believe it was evident he was correct as I watched blind eyes open, legs grow out, backs healed, demons cast out, and the dead raised through his ministry. Something heavenly must have been in the room!

Have you ever been in a service and all of a sudden it feels as though the atmosphere changes. There is a shift and you can feel an increase of God's presence? I believe that sometimes when this takes place it is because that an angelic being has entered the room. They have been in the very presence of God and they are now in the same room as you! The residual effect is happening. The anointing that they have basked in, in heaven, they have now spread to you as they entered the room. They have entered into your space to bring healing, deliverance, prophetic words, and blessings from the Father. I know not all Christiandom accepts or even believe in angels ministering with the heirs of salvation. I actually sat in a service one time where the preacher was talking about being careful when it comes to angels. He said you don't want to start looking for angels. While he was stating his negative view on the angels I had Jesus speaking in my ear very clearly. Here is what He had to say on the subject. "How dare a man criticize my creation? I have created him lower than the angels. Who is he to say how my kingdom shall work." I felt the anger of the Lord at this minister who thought he had it all figured out. The scripture says, "What is man, that thou art mindful of him? Or the son of man that thou visitest him? [7] *Thou madest him a little lower than the angels;" Hebrews 2:6-7. My word on the subject of angels is this: If you don't believe God uses angels you are limiting your ministry and your life to only what you can understand. At some point you must discern "who is happening" if you can't discern "what is happening". And when you discern it is God then you must have enough wisdom to take your hand off of it even if you don't understand it.*

Angels of Traveling Mercies

Once as we were traveling back to Missouri from Texas, I looked out the window and I saw a huge angel. It was probably the largest I have ever seen. He was flying beside us with his head in the wind. He turned and looked at me as he continued flying. His head was as large as our vehicle. I felt comforted knowing our travel was very much protected!

It will startle you when you first start seeing angels. It is natural to jump when you see them because you are seeing something that is not normally seen. So you may gasp or *jump, that is fine until you get used to seeing them. Now if you encounter one and fear comes over you, not a startle, but a fear, then the being isn't a Godly one. You have the power to rebuke it in the name of Jesus!*

I have had people want me to pray so that they can see angels. They say they want to see angels but nothing evil or demonic. You can't have the one without the other. If you see who is for you, you will also see who is against you. That's a rephrase of the 2 Kings 6:17 (KJV), "And Elisha prayed, and said, LORD, I pray thee, open his eyes, that he may see. And the LORD opened the eyes of the young man; and he saw: and, behold, the mountain was full of horses and chariots of fire round about Elisha".

Being a "seer" you will see good and you will see bad. I was praying for people in a prayer line and as I was fixing to lay my hands on a young lady in the line all of a sudden I could see a demon setting on her head curled around her head riding her. My instinct was to pull my hand back. So after the initial surprise I went ahead and placed my hand on her. She was set free in the name of Jesus! You have to learn to condition your spiritual man to function regardless of what you see knowing that greater is He that is within you than he that is in the world. 1 John 4:4 ...."greater is he that is in you, then he that is in the world".

Children and their Heavenly abilities

I honestly believe children are naturally spiritual seers from birth. They have just left the Kingdom of heaven where all things a supernatural to come here on earth to fulfill what God has planned for their life to accomplish. They are seers until we fleshly adults tell them they can't see. Then they tend to start losing the abilities from heaven as we pound into them, "no, you didn't see anything". Makes you wonder how much better our children could walk before God successfully if we didn't program them to be unspiritual beings. The bible says that when referring to children, "such is the Kingdom of heaven." "But Jesus said,

Suffer little children, and forbid them not, to come unto me: for of such is the kingdom of heaven." King James Version Matthew 19:14

One of the best prophetic sessions we have ever had was when about 3 children around the ages of 9-11 years set across from us at a meeting. We had signed up for a session where you would go in and set down at a table. You were not to say anything while the ones across the table from you prayed. After they prayed they would tell you what God had showed them about you. At this session three children set across from us and read our mail! What they had seen in the spirit was right on. So to that I say train your child up to see and hear in the spirit. Never tell them they can't see or that God does not speak. God does speak we just aren't listening.

This is not the End there is more,

so much more to come!

Made in the USA
Monee, IL
06 March 2021